Junior Artist

by Richard C. Lawrence
illustrated by N. Kanayama

MODERN CURRICULUM PRESS
Pearson Learning Group

Kimmy liked to listen to the morning announcements. Her best friend, Deb, was the one who read them. Kimmy thought that Deb had the most beautiful voice in the school. Deb was so calm and independent! It didn't matter to Deb that the whole school could hear her. It would matter to me, Kimmy thought.

"Good morning, students," said the voice. Deb announced something about a bake sale and something about Parent-Teacher Week. Then she announced something that really made Kimmy sit up and pay attention.

"Local artist Nick Christopher is going to paint a mural on the north wall of our school. As part of the project, he is going to choose a student to help him. If you think you might be interested, pick up an application in the office."

Kimmy had always dreamed of being a painter. Walking home, she said to Deb, "Being an artist must be the greatest thing in the world."

"You ought to get that application from the office," Deb said.

Kimmy was silent.

"What's the matter?" Deb asked.

"I don't know. What if he doesn't pick me? And what if he does? Maybe he'll think he picked the wrong kid. And I don't want to work outside where people will be watching. Rejection and criticism make me feel bad."

"You're the most qualified person I know," Deb told her. "Everyone knows you're the best artist in the school. And Nick Christopher needs a student to work with him. The city council told him he should have one. I really think you should fill out that application."

The next day, Kimmy went to the office and asked, "Where are the applications for that art project?"

The secretary pointed to a stack of papers on the counter. They were blank sheets!

"I think he wants you to draw something," the secretary said.

Nervously, Kimmy picked up a sheet of paper. She had no idea what to draw for this application. She was really afraid of getting rejected.

She took the application home. Just before bed, she had an idea. She drew her dream school. She drew fountains with wild animals drinking in them. In her dream school, there were murals on every wall.

"No one will like this," she said. "It's too weird."

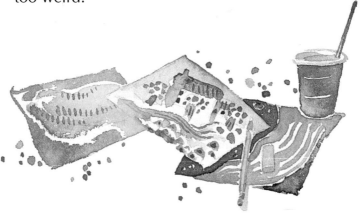

Two weeks later, during the morning announcements, Deb's voice said, "And we're very pleased to say that sixth-grader Kimberly Postman has been chosen to assist artist Nick Christopher in painting the mural on the north wall of the school. Way to go, Kimmy! We knew you were qualified. Here's to your successful job application!"

Kimmy gasped with joy. "He picked me!" she shouted, without thinking.

Everyone turned and looked at her. Kimmy was so embarrassed! She slumped down in her chair.

Kimmy was nervous when she went to meet Nick Christopher. Her mother drove her to the artist's downtown studio—a big loft with high ceilings. Paintings stood against the walls. Most of the paintings were huge. More paintings hung on the walls. Some of them weren't finished yet. One of them was just a blank canvas. In one corner was a wooden table with a drawing pad, pencils and charcoals, and a clip-on lamp. In another corner stood long, thin strips of wood and an easel.

"Those are stretchers for canvas," Nick explained. "I form four stretchers into a rectangle. Then I staple the canvas onto the wood."

"Staples? I thought you're supposed to use tacks," she said. Nick laughed, and she blushed.

"I'm glad you know so much about painting," he said. "Now, when you work for me, you're going to have to do two opposite things. You have to follow my directions. But you also have to be independent. You have to work well by yourself, solve problems, and have creative ideas. Can you do all that?"

"I think so," Kimmy said uncertainly.

That fall and winter, Kimmy visited Nick's studio after school, for two hours a day, twice a week. Nick was a friendly man with a soft voice. He enjoyed big sandwiches, iced tea, and books about famous artists.

Nick taught her about mixing, thickening, and thinning paints. He taught her different ways to use a roller and a brush. He also showed her how to drip paint onto a canvas from a hole in the bottom of a tin can. Nick showed her a dozen different reds, four different whites, and a million different grays. He showed her how the same shade of green would look darker next to one color and lighter next to another. He showed her that a shadow on a person's face has many different colors in it. He told her about artists like Picasso, Matisse, Van Eyck, and Rembrandt.

Soon she was actually helping him. She held the fresh canvas tight when he stapled it to the wooden stretchers. She poured a little more white or a little more black into a color to make it lighter or darker, and he asked her whether it looked right. She was becoming an independent thinker.

"Which of these designs for the mural do you like best?" Nick asked.

Kimmy looked at the four sketches on Nick's drafting table. All of them showed the history of the town. Aside from that, they were quite different.

Kimmy studied them closely for a long time. "This one," she said finally. The design she liked best showed the main street of the town as a time line. On the left were the Native Americans hunting in the woods, then the early European settlers clearing land for farms. From left to right, she could see the town growing as time passed. A railroad arrived, then cars and planes. On the far right, the people of the town walked into the future.

"Great," Nick said. "Then that's the one we'll use."

When spring came, it was time to paint the mural. Kimmy spent many afternoons with Nick shopping for art supplies and carrying things. At the art supply store, she helped carry big cans of paint into Nick's van. She had never seen so much paint before.

"I'm using very high-quality paint, so the mural will last for years in the wind and rain," Nick said. "Luckily the city council is paying for it!"

efore they could paint, they needed to clean the wall. Nick and Kimmy took off all the dirt with soap, water, and a wire brush. They filled every crack with plaster to make the wall smooth. After the plaster dried, they covered a portion of the wall with white paint.

Nick already had drawn the mural on paper. That was called a cartoon. Now it was time to draw the full-size picture on the wall.

Nick divided the cartoon into squares. He divided the school wall into larger squares. Then he copied each square of the cartoon onto a larger square on the wall. That way, he could be sure all the parts of the picture fit together.

Nick painted with large brushes. He started from the upper left corner of the wall. First he painted one square. Then he painted another. Because he was starting at the top, his clothes didn't rub against any of the wet paint.

It was Kimmy's job to give Nick the right brush for the color he was using. At the end of each day, Kimmy cleaned the brushes and stored them in big cans to dry. Before long, she was painting backgrounds on the mural.

ownspeople came by to see the mural as it was being painted. Friends, teachers, and parents stopped and asked questions. Kimmy was happier than she had ever been.

She thought to herself, "I'm painting out in the open where everyone can see me! And it's not bothering me!"

Kimmy's parents looked at the mural almost every afternoon. They hugged her and said, "You're doing a great job!"

When the mural was mostly done, Nick said to Kimmy, "I think it's about time you painted more than just backgrounds, don't you?"

He showed her which square of wall to paint independently. He pointed out the paints and brushes he wanted her to use. She painted carefully, within the lines Nick had drawn on the wall. She felt as if a great artist were guiding her hand.

Her square came out very well! Nick asked her to paint another one. With two painters, the mural grew quickly.

When the mural was finished, the city council gave a party. Then it was time to give the picture its finishing touch. It was time for the artist to sign his name.

Nick Christopher signed his name in big, curly letters in the bottom right corner of the mural. Then Nick handed a brush to Kimmy.

"This was a two-person job," he said. "You sign too."

Kimmy could hardly believe it. As long as the mural lasted on the wall, her name would be there as one of the artists.

She painted her name at the very bottom, under Nick's. When she turned around to put her brush away, the whole school was cheering for her.

"Thank you for believing in me," Kimmy said to Nick.

"And thank you for being the best junior artist I've ever had," he answered.